The Foo

Jesus Footprints in the Sand

American Poet

Carolyn Joyce Carty

The Footprints of My Heart

Need I say you are the beginning of my life

My soul and the footprints of my heart

I am there for you, no not just a wondering star

You are the beginning of my soul you are its end

For you my love I am here, my light is yours

Leave me not at your door; bear the greeting of my heart

If I could tell you the secrets of my heart

Say you will carry me, for the sake of love

You shall go and keep your eyes upon my heart

To bring a hope again; I took upon the world

A knee to all across the world

Till the night you call my name

I will look upon the footprints of my heart

I know we have a destiny in everything we do

I dreamed the crossing of my heart

Need I know my destiny I hoped that I could tell you

Once I dreamed a dream of you, I dreamed you'd say

You are the beginning of my life, my soul

And the footprints of my heart

Thou Art My Joy

Thou art my joy,

My hope, my trust,

My youth

Thou art you

Who brought me forth

From my mother's womb

Oh, be not far from me with grace

I will tell them of your righteous act

Proclaim to them your wondrous deeds

Blessed be your glorious name

Truly, God is good to those pure of heart

May you be the rain itself that showers the waters upon the earth and deliver them that need

They will call upon your name

Oppressed no more, but free

Thou art my hope,

My trust, Thou art my joy, my youth

The Fruit of Experience of Mankind

Dedicated to Robert Louis Scharring-Hausen

My Publisher & Great Uncle

Historian Founding Father of Library Week

Hopewell, New Jersey May 1921

"Oh you who seek me

I am the Fruit of Experience of Mankind

Is learning dearly taught

Seek not the treasures of my libraries

Seek My Thoughts

In books one talks of wise men

In life one walks with Kings"

Footprints

One night I had a dream. I dreamed I was walking along the beach with the Lord. Across the sky flashed scenes from my life. For each scene, I noticed two sets of footprints in the sand. One belonging to me and the other to the Lord

When the last scene of my life flashed before me, I looked back at the footprints in the sand. I noticed that many times along the path of my life there was only one set of footprints. I also noticed that it happened at the very lowest and saddest times of my life.

This really bothered me and I questioned the Lord about it. "Lord you said that once I decided to follow you, you'd walk with me all the way. However, I have noticed that during the most troublesome times in my life there is only one set of footprints. I don't understand why when I needed you most you would leave me."

The Lord replied, "My precious, precious child, I love you and I would never leave you! During your times of trial and suffering when you see only one set of footprints, it was then that I carried you."

The Footprints of God

I found myself in the midst of God and all of whom are with him. His guardian cherubim angel, protecting the tree of life with his brilliant sword swiftly moving in all directions.

Lest He put forth his hand, ye shall not partake of the tree of life. Only those who can announce it from these things of old can let it be told.

His love was as it was in the beginning. He is the Lord who has made all things, who stretched out the heavens alone, who told this long ago. God is with you, there is no other, no other God besides him.

Who is like him, let him proclaim it, let him declare it and set it forth before him.

Only those who can announce it from these things of old can let it be told. Lest he put forth his hand that ye shall partake of the tree of life, then and only then can you live forever.

Who is like him, let him proclaim it, let him declare it and set forth before him. Let it be told, fear not, has he not told ye from of old, the gift of wings, the gift of the sand and the seas.

The gift, who are you, where have you come from, where are you going. I am a writer's inkhorn that stands beside the sea. As a child, I was spiritually guided into this life, for only reasons myself and my maker can understand.

I have come from the unknown facets of the footprints on the sands of time. To me, the light of life has been here before and will be here again only lead your spirit with understanding and contentment.

The spirit that dwells in me is of love and peace. My purpose was to grow and learn based on the light of love. I brought with me a gift. For my spirit was of a chosen one, happy that I be a product of my maker.

As a girl, allow me to enchant you with the beauty of the light of my eye. For it is in the light of my eye that will allow you to find the mystery of Gods glory. Follow the light of love and it will be made known unto you.

O Lord if I could give you the sun and the moon, would you seek the secret of my soul? For even a star could fall upon or rise beyond horizons. My words shall rise beyond my words. If I could be a star I would encounter the sky, but for the day that I have come to you, I seek not to be a star, I seek to be a child, a child, a light.

So it is the inquiry, a man of the field or revelry. Given a Prince a birthright too, two manners of people, separate, two nations born of thee, so is a man; a revelry.

Like a silent raindrop or a shower in the rain, there will be my memories, shall my voice be still, and my words shall drop as rain. As my generation, as my grandfather, as my father before thee, to remember mercy of thy people, just and right are we all way to find truth without iniquity.

And so it is that I will love with greatness and you shall be my rock. A man of the field inherits a nation, while and eagle stirreth up her flock youth will spread its wings. And I say that to you who are born of the mountains, I say pray to the mountain. And to you who are born to the seas, I say pray to the sea. And to you who are born to the tree of life, I say pray to thee. And to you who are born of the light, I say pray to his light.

And if a day shall come to you that you may seek to gather his light then let us be joined. For all living things, have a purpose but the voice of the Lord and the wind whisper a song. his song, my word, his word, the word of love.

O Lord sometimes I dreamed these dreams, and at times I desired such desires, desires that I wished to share with you an uncommon love among most, the spirit of his holy host.

For I would rather that I rise into a cloud than to be a star only to encounter the sky. For your love is a rhythm that can always be counted. One can count the drops of water that can rise up and fall upon its shores.

Encompass only what is felt in your heart. Perceive not to fulfill thyself, perceive enchantment, enchantment of his song. His song, a song as fast as the sea, remembering in your dreams, dreams that keep yourself with love.

For it is not the beauty of your being that has attracted me to you. It is the depth of your soul. It is the depth of your eyes, your spirit and your smile. It is where you placed your kiss upon me when we first met.

I closed my eyes, I cherish that moment, a moment in time, and I shall whisper the words he so dearly wished to hear. For when I closed my eyes, I saw the universe and when I opened them, I saw love. I saw love being free and totally in awe of being He.

If my word reached, you not then have this understanding that I had stumbled upon thy word, stumble not for his words have not yet fallen.

O Lord your love binds me. If all I have said is truth than truth shall reveal itself. Think not that I say these words so one can say I praise you well. I only see the good in you. I only speak to you in words that you yourselves know in loving thought.

Wise men had come unto you to give you wisdom. And I have come unto you to give you wisdom and to walk in this wisdom also. For I have found truth. It is the spirit of God the spirit of his love. It is the spirit of his guardian cherubim of wings.

Hold my hand with might and envision in your heart understanding love. Do not judge by the sight of your eyes. Neither reprove the hearing of your ears for your thoughts shall be pure and the spirit of the Lord shall rest upon you.

The spirit of His love and faith, the spirit of His wisdom and understanding,. the spirit of His counsel, the spirit of His strength, his might. The spirit of this knowledge is the spirit of the Lord.

By the strength of his hand, he had done these things and by the strength of my hand, I will show you these things.

More so, by my strength, which is his wisdom, he has yet to gather all in the earth and yet there was only one that could move his wings. For his righteousness was written upon you and his faithfulness was upon you also

What man shall be among you that have one sheep! And if it falls into a pit, will he not lay hold on to it to lift it out! How much then is a man better than a sheep!

For what manner of a man is this that he commanded, even the wind, the waters, the seas, and they obeyed him. For he has the power to pick it up and he has the power to lay it back down again.

Let us then, go up at once and possess it, for we are well able to receive him. For he was drawn into the wilderness as He sent the multitudes away, He went up upon a mountain apart and there he prayed and the evening had come to pass and he was there alone.

Yeah he did walk, that his wings might be spread upon the good earth and for all that is done that it be done in his good name. And that your love may be peaceable and nurturing. Oh and that with all your might, that your might, might turn him.

He goes to the east and to the west. He goes to the north and to the south and yes, his love, is always there. Therefore find comfort one to another in his words. Hold fast to that which is good. For the very God of Peace is not the author of confusion, he sanctifies you.

Faithful is He that calleth you for some have departed in faith. Blessed are the eyes, which see these things that you may see. For it is a joyful thing to fall into the hands of the "Living God" and believe thee in ye for I am in all knowing

What man shall be among you that have one sheep! How much then is a man better than his sheep! For he leaded me to his waters & tempted me not and neither did he forsake me

For I am in remembrance, remembrance of Our Father. Speak for the years that have been hidden in your face. My longing of the cloud, the depth of the dream, who had closed their eyes for God is Love.

When the storm passes, Proclaim the lightening of His Majesty. Behold God is my salvation. I do trust and will not be afraid. He is my strength, my song. And His light shall be like a fire and His Holy One a flame.

And it shall consume the glory of His tree of life. The fruitful fields of both body and soul. And the rest of the trees shall be few, that a child, his guardian Cherubim angel might write your name.

And it shall come to pass that God's seeds shall be mighty and shall stay upon the earth. The only one, the Holy one, a truth and so it is the spirit of his wings.

Woe unto them that decree unrighteous decree and that which write grievousness which have been prescribed. To turn aside the needy from judgment and that take away the right from the poor.

For all this, there is anger and it is not turned away, His hand is stretched out still. Praised and blessed is man that fears and delights greatly in Him. For his seas are mighty. The generation of the upright shall be blessed.

And to the upright, there arises light in darkness for this He is gracious and full of compassion. His heart is established. He sees His desires, His righteousness endures forever. His Horn is exalted with Honor. He is a glorious and shining light and we shall be willing for all seasons to rejoice in His light.

There is another that bears witness of me and I know that the witness of me is true. For I receive not testimony from man for these things I say, that you might see and that you might be saved.

Verily a time shall come to you that you may seek to hear the voice of the son of God the son of man. And they that hear shall live. Behold that which I have seen for God answers in the joy of His heart.

For He is a God at hand and not a God far off, behold He is against them that prophesy false dreams. For if, they had stood at his counsel they would have had cause to have heard these words.

And they that stand still may despise me, yet I shall have peace. And for anyone that walks after his imagination of his own heart, there shall stand a counselor that has marked these words. Could anyone therefore hide himself! I think not and so say it is the word. How long shall it be in the hearts of the hands of those that deceive?

For they have deceived their own hearts. Think not that I have cause to forget their names. For their names shall come to my dreams in His words.

Is not my word his rock that is his peace! For the vision was in giving to all nations. As for His beauty, He is in Majesty every man according to his image in the chamber of His imagery.

Yet I had sat weeping, my eye shall not spare nor have pity, though they cry in my ears that a voice will not hear them. I am a writer's inkhorn that stands beside the sea. Let not an eye neither spare nor have pity for there appeared a form of a man that held the gift of wings.

And everyone went straight way, everyone I did see. As for them whose heart walks after his heart, so the vision that I had seen went up from me and it was He who showed me these.

And he said that I shall teach the difference between holy and profane and cause them to discern for themselves. Blessed and holy is he who enters into sanctity and there shall be his tablet to minister and to be ministered.

And he said, "Sanctify Gods love for I am in remembrance of my father." How be it that He made known unto me this revelation. For the vision was of one man that lent not his wings to another

If my word reached you not, then have this understanding that I had stumbled upon thy word, stumble not for His words have not yet fallen.

Whose hand is to be laid upon you! Whose hand is to be your honor! Is a shepherd not joyful to breathe, to tremble! Who shall be mindful! Who shall wear the mark of a King!

For what is it to rise and cease breathing! For what is it to die or to stand alone in the wind! For the voice that weaved this cloud shall lift its voice. Your eyes, your eyes will see. Your ears, your ears will hear. Your heart, your heart will be one with your mind in awe of loving you forevermore.

Tell this vision to all mankind because of your belief, he said unto me to tell thee. "If ye only have faith as once was said to the mountain and nothing shall be impossible to thee." What thinketh thou that the King of the earth does rise! Then and only then you shall be free. Trust that your face beholds thy father for He had come to save the world that which had been lost.

And He said unto me, "If two or more of you shall gather together for anything that they shall ask, to them it shall be given." As for men that could not receive this saying, "Save they to whom it was given." For there are those who are born of Enoch's, which have made themselves receivers of His Kingdom.

As for Him who is able to receive, let him receive, for there is only one God that calleth you good. And as His voice whispered in the wind, he said unto me, "If it be thy will enter into life and keep thy commandments, give to the poor and thou shall have all the treasures of thee."

For you see with man this seemed impossible, but with God all things are possible and for anyone that had forsaken all things that are they that are shall inherit all things. "For it is lawful for me to do with, for what is mine." For many were truly called, yet only one is truly called and chosen. Ye shall indeed drink of His cup as to sit on the left side or to the right is not mine to say, it is not mine to give, yet it is earned of him to whom you truly have ministered.

And it is given that who-so-ever be chieftain among you; he shall surely be thy servant, of perseverance. Therefore, He said unto me, "If ye have faith and doubt not, ye shall not only do that which is told ye, ye shall do that which is done to the fig tree and to the olives and to the vineyard and also that which is done to the mountain as it shall be."

For all things which ye ask of are in prayer and for all things which ye receive are answered and received in prayer and then given. Neither have I told you by what authority I know these things.

Neither I tell you by what authority I do these things, but think what you may of a certain man.

I am a writer's inkhorn that stands beside the sea. How long have ye wondered that the number of his children be like the sand and the sea. For there it was once said to those that are his people. And for those who seek, some shall keep, some shall find peace, some shall find shame, some shall find contempt, some shall find an everlasting life and they that are wise shall shine brightly.

For my father's voice woed unto me, and it woed wisdom. His image graved and silenced, his words a sword! Their days are numbered said he and so it is that he said it with love. O Lord, O love, so love is still upon me and so is the spirit of his wings that he might carry you.

Does not wisdom call, does not understanding praise his voice on the heights besides his waters. In the Lords path, I took my stand beside thee. His gate a part of me, beside him side by side, I cried aloud woe.

To my father and to you I called and my voice was to the son of God. O dear ones, walk with love, walk with him, and love prudence. For if, I have been foolish, and then I shall be wise. For noble things were said and from my lips will yield what is right.

For I only uttered truth and wickedness will not yield my thoughts. For all the words of his sword are righteous, they are all straight to him who understands and right to those who find his knowledge.

Heed His knowledge rather than to chose silver or gold. For wisdom is better than to be a fool. And not all that you desire can compare. For the Lord Desires wisdom with prudence and for that I found His knowledge.

For fear of the Lord, pride and arrogance are the ways that pervert speech. He held counsel for wisdom. He held insight for strength. For Kings have reigned by them and rulers do decreed what is just.

A Prince who rules among nobles are they who truly govern and they that walk amongst us, so say it is the word. Sow it to those who sayeth the Lord in the name of Christ Jesus.

He only loves those who love him. And for those who sought him diligently, found Him. From when the heavens were made, he was there. And when he drew a circle on the face of the deep, even as he made the skies as the foundations of the deep had been established he was there.

And as he assigned the seas to its limits so that the water might not transgress his commandments it is then that we were then marked out of the very foundations of the heavens to the good earth.

It was then that I was beside him, a Prince among the sand and the sea. Daily I walked in his light, rejoicing and delighting with him always, rejoicing and delighting for mankind.

So to the son of God and to the sons of man hear my voice, listen to me, for his will is our will. For happy are those who keep his ways. For his fruits are better than gold.

He walked in the path of righteousness. He walked in the path of justices. He had endowed me with wealth and for those who truly loved him. He had fulfilled the treasures for your hearts and your minds and for your souls.

When the Lord had created me in the beginning, it was one of his first acts of old. He continually kept watch over me. Ages ago, before the beginnings of the good earth, when there were no depths, I was then brought forth.

And when the springs had yet abound His waters, before the hills and the mountains were yet formed, I was yet to be born. I was then brought forth, before he made the earth with His fields, His first dust of the world and His first fruits.

I took heed to his instructions to be wise, not to neglect myself. Happy is man who may listen. He will take watch daily over his gate. He will wait beside his door. And for those who seek him they will find him they will find life, they will find his love. By that, you will obtain true favor of the Lord. Only He who misses him may endure. And for all that is his love one cannot compare. Trusts in the Lord with all your heart, in all ways, always acknowledge Him.

For straight is His path in all ways that He has made ye. Therefore, I have told ye, that from heaven we are born and from the dust we are brought to the sea. And from the sea, we are born to the sand and from the sand to His breath; we are brought to His feet.

And as He walked upon the good earth, so shall we. How long have ye wondered that the number of His children be like the sand and the sea. And it was in his own voice that he had made himself known; now all your longing is now known. My sighs are hidden not, yes I pray, I am like a man, it is he who had a dream, and in the name of the dear Lord Christ Jesus certain was his dream.

Pray for them, for they shall trust,

That they shall have a good conscience

In all things willing

To live and love honestly

And that they may walk towards them

Towards those that are without,

And that they may have lack of nothing

For what is our hope,

Our joy for others

That the just do live by faith

And by believing in me

Believe in the saving of the soul.

For what is our hope, our joy for others

That faith is the substance

Of all things hoped for.

For what is the hope, the joy

For the glory of the word of the Lord,

This day as it is each and every day

The footprints of his faith

For it was written upon Him in the name of the Father from above for all man "to see the fellowship of mankind." It was His song of the night of the sand and the sea. For was it not written upon the tablets of your hearts that through Him man shall be forever upright.

And for those who inhabit the earth that all humankind shall be forever upright and all men of integrity will remain in it. How long dear Lord that it is that I have cried out for thee.

For He had worked a Foot in your day that you should believe on, and it is this, these are the true footprints of His eternal inheritance.

For He was a Lamb, and the first-born was to guide them to their feet, into the way of Peace, to fill the tablets of your hearts. So say ye, fill the tablets of His heart. Let no man go unadorned by Him.

One cannot trodden His city that is built which has the foundations whose builder and maker is God. While looking unto Jesus, the pioneer and perfector of all faith, who for the very joy that was set forth before him, endured.

For it is he, who is seated at the right hand of God, a great quake set forth and it summoned him, His guardian cherubim of glory over shadowed him praising and sayings, "Thou art thy God, Thou art thy God alone of whom you were told of these things of old, to greet the perfector of your faith in Christ Jesus, with one foot love and with one foot peace."

And it is so that you may gather round with Him and all of whom that are with Him.

O Lord, place upon their face to shine and set aside their wings, incline their ears to hear and open up their eyes, open up their hearts to sing. You will call them one by one, call them by their name. My love for you is still the same that I might carry them for you up on thy holy hill.

What is my name! What shall I say to them, the Who I am. It is I, who say this, who am I to He, who it is that sent me, that is my name forever. I am a child, a child of God. I had stretched out my hand and I wrote with all that is wondrous. And wherever I go, you shall not be empty, you will believe on in me.

The Lord is God, God is with you and there is no other, no other God beside Him. The zeal of the Lord of Host did say this. He said, "I the Lord the first and with the last I am He" and as He sat upon His throne and kept watch over His Kingdom to establish and uphold it with justice and righteousness from this time forth and forevermore.

One cannot eat of the Tree of Knowledge, for when ye take part of that which is both good and evil, in that day that you eat of it surely your soul will die. However, when man washes clean His heart, man becomes like one unto Him knowing the difference of good and evil.

Lest He put forth His hand only and take part with one-foot love and the other peace and takes part only in that which is good, then and only then can ye take part also of the tree of life, the true footprints of his eternal inheritance.

For having endured in faith and love and by asking in forgiveness in the name of the dear Lord, that Ye may receive of the Tree of Life and does eat so that you may live forever and ever and forevermore.

For every man that shall sit under his tree, none shall make you afraid. For the Lord of Host has spoken for all who walk in His name. There is no end of treasure or wealth of every precious thing, Abide by Him that he may carry you upon his precious wings.

One night a man had a dream, the night then turned to day. With one-foot love with one-foot peace, he then began to pray for the love of mankind to walk all the way for the grace of love and peace of the dear Lord Christ Jesus to be with all men. And for all that is His love, only one can compare.

For His sword passes quickly and moves swiftly, moving in all directions, remembering these things of old. Who has stretched out his hand alone and wrote with all that is wondrous.

He is the Lord who has made all things, who stretched out the heavens above. Who is like Him, Let him Proclaim it, Let him declare it and set forth before Him. Let it be told, fear not, has he not told ye from of old, the gift of wings, the gifts of the sand and the sea.

When I bring you good news or news of great joy for that which does come for all people to see so will the sword of His word that will pierce your very soul, that your thoughts will be revealed in his heart

And you will be called first-born to guide them to their feet into the way of peace to fill their hearts. For the hand of the Lord was upon me. The Lord our God, the Lord as one, a day God called the chosen.

For it He, who is the Prince of Peace, who makes us whole, who abolished their faith, the law is the law; One Lord, one faith, one God, just as you were truly called, to bring hope to one in all, speak truth, put away falsehoods. Labor honestly with your hands so that you may be able to help those in need.

Be alive in Him through your every precious word and your every precious deeds conducting oneself wisely. Be gracious and in self-control. Reach to all nations. Believe on in the word and the world. Hold on the armor that which is God.

May you have the power to comprehend to know the love of knowledge that has been passed to you, just as you were truly called to one hope, for we are all members of one another! Be wise walk in love. Surely, the world is worthy and full of acceptance to keep alive and together the Footprints of God.

God made ye and every living thing thereof. He made the sun and the moon. He made the heavens and the earth and all that are in it. Glory is to God. For God blesses you, as I do also, for does thou know from whence they came, indeed you do. For God blessed you and me and multiplied all of our descendants as the stars of the heavens and as the sand of the sea. Take my hand, take his wings. Footprints in the sand and the sea,

Footprints in the sand from my hand, take his wings. For long life is in my right hand and in my left is Honor. "May all your ways be in pleasantness and all your paths always peace."

Written by Carolyn Joyce Carty a child prodigy 1963

Jesus Footprints in the Sand

One night a man had a dream. He dreamed He was walking along the beach with the Lord. Across the sky flashed scenes from his life. For each scene, he noticed two sets of footprints in the sand. One belonging to him and the other to the Lord

When the last scene of his life flashed before him he looked back at the footprints in the sand. He noticed that many times along the path of his life there was only one set of footprints. He also noticed that it happened at the very lowest and saddest times of my life.

This really bothered him and he questioned the Lord about it. "Lord you said that once I decided to follow you, you'd walk with me all the way. However, I have noticed that during the most troublesome times in my life there is only one set of footprints. I don't understand why when I needed you most you would leave me."

The Lord replied, "My precious, precious child, I love you and I would never leave you! During your times of trial and suffering when you see only one set of footprints, it was then that I carried you."

Author Anonymous Carolyn Joyce Carty © Copyright

Who were author anonymous most famous unknown authors who wrote the poem Footprints? Ella H. Scharring-Hausen, Princeton Educator and Sunday School Teacher wrote the original Footprints in the Sand poem on June 6, 1922.

Its first line read; one night I dreamed I was walking along the beach with the Lord. Ella H. Scharring-Hausen's poem is now public domain property according to the copyright law of 1909. The Footprints in the Sand poem was later rewritten with permission by its owner on April Passion Week 1963 by Ella H. Scharring-Hausen's great niece, Carolyn Joyce Carty a six year old.

The Footprints poem famous first line then became, one night a man had a dream. This first line was written by Robert Louis Scharring-Hausen, writer, editor, author, nature columnist and Founding Father of Library Week from Hopewell, New Jersey 1921.

Carolyn Joyce Carty revised the entire text in 1963 into its present form, which has become known as the more popular version of the Footprints poem.

The original Footprints in the Sand poem were written by Ella H Scharring-Hausen in 1922 at the age of 28. The rewritten version of Footprints poem was then written on an old Remington typewriter, it was written in one of Hopewell, New Jersey's finest Historical Homes located on Moore's Mill Road.

Footprints were written by the six-year old child prodigy who could read and write well at the age of four. Carolyn Joyce Carty wrote Footprints in 1963; Carolyn was often called Carrie Jo which was a derivative of her given name. The word Carrie was then underlined in the original poem and was used as her anonymous signature.

The Historical Home where Footprints was written belonged to Robert Louis & Ella H. Scharring-Hausen. Ella Scharring-Hausen taught school in Princeton. Robert Louis Scharring-Hausen was a farmer and a nature columnist and wrote for the Trenton Times.

Robert & Ella Scharring-Hausen were neighbors and friends with other Historians such as Charles Lindberg & Anne Morrow Lindbergh. They were neighbors to the Schwarzkopf's and the Guttenberg's all of Hopewell, New Jersey.

The Scharring-Hausen's often entertained quest from Princeton New Jersey such as Albert Einstein, John Fitzgerald Kennedy, and Dr. Linus Pauling all Nobel hopefuls.

Robert & Ella Scharring-Hausen & a group called "The Roundabouts" helped found and erect the Hopewell Museum and Library in Hopewell, New Jersey 1921-1922.

For more historical information please visit the Hopewell Museum & Hopewell Library located in Hopewell, New Jersey to enjoy the founder's legacy.

These individuals were Philanthropist and were the first group of people in the U. S. Nation to form Library Week in Hopewell, New Jersey, the third week of May in 1922. A play called "Help Hopewell Honor Her Hero" also known as "The Masque of Hopewell" was written by Robert Louis Scharring-Hausen.

The play was based on The Founding Father of the U.S. Nation George Washington, crossing the Delaware River. The proceeds from the Play were used to establish the Hopewell Museum in Honor of the Late Sarah D. Stout and her collection of fine antiques. The collection of fine antiques, were then displayed, at the Museum, which remains today.

All three individual names appeared on the copyrights of Footprints also known as Footprints in the Sand. They are authors Robert Louis Scharring-Hausen, Carolyn Joyce Carty & Ella H. Scharring-Hausen.

Its authorship was listed as an Anonymous Contribution to Society. Footprints were copyrighted in the He and I text. No other author's text supports or substantiates any other version of copyright or use. Although many have claimed to write the Footprints poem for personal gain or notoriety, none can compare with the original collection written in 1963 while each author remained alive.

Robert Louis Scharring-Hausen's writings are preserved in archives; some remain at Rutgers University in New Jersey. Scholarships for journalism were funded and founded to Rutgers University upon the passing of Ella H. Scharring-Hausen in 1984.

Carolyn Joyce Carty, (Carrie) is currently in publishing still sharing her writings with humankind and charitable & faithful organizations and individuals.

The Footprints of God is the short story that belongs to the Footprints poem. The short story written by Carolyn Joyce Carty was solely based from Bible lesson teachings that Ella H. Scharring-Hausen's often shared with her Sunday school students.

All poetry written was based on Bible verses & text to promote faith, philosophy and philanthropy towards humankind without solace to promote any individual or denominational preferences. All faiths are encouraged to share these universal thoughts, its unity of love & peace.

Carolyn Joyce Carty received Editor's Choice Award for Outstanding Achievement in Poetry, for her poems titled Faith & the Thirst of Christ. Carolyn Joyce Carty was recently nominated Best Poet for her poems titled Faith & Behold My Heart. Carolyn Joyce Carty would most like to be remembered as a passion writer and the youngest philanthropist there has ever been. Enjoy God's gift of faith and please share your love of Footprints.

Special Thanks to:

Robert Louis Scharring-Hausen Nature Columnist 1963, Historic Founding Father of Library Week 1922 from Hopewell, New Jersey, Publisher & Rutgers University Graduate.

Ella H. Scharring-Hausen Princeton educator and Sunday school teacher who wrote the original Footprints in the Sand poem less popular version on June 6, 1922. These collections of writings were used to inspire this poetry from Ella's Sunday school teaching lessons.

A special thanks to all who love the Footprints Poetry Anthology Literary Classic Collector's Edition. The truth is there are only one set of the Footprints poem. The Author Anonymous version has often been mistaken for Author Unknown.

The genuine version of Footprints is; one night a man had a dream. Others have claimed, one night I dreamed a dream, and one night I dreamed a dream that I was walking were public domain versions later claimed by numerous authors. Ella H. Scharring-Hausen declared her none popular versions public domain in 1968 upon the death of her late husband Robert Louis Scharring-Hausen.

Author Anonymous version has become known as the more popular version by far and is copyrighted intellectual property owned by Carolyn Joyce Carty and is not public domain.

Footprints

One night a man had a dream. He dreamed He was walking along the beach with the Lord. Across the sky flashed scenes from his life. For each scene, He noticed two sets of footprints in the sand. One belonging to him and the other to the Lord

When the last scene of his life flashed before him He looked back at his footprints in the sand. He noticed that many times along the path of his life there was only one set of footprints. He also noticed that it happened at the very lowest and saddest times of his life.

This really bothered him and He questioned the Lord about it. "Lord you said that once I decided to follow you, you'd walk with me all the way. However, I have noticed that during the most troublesome times in my life there is only one set of footprints. I don't understand why when I needed you most you would leave me."

The Lord replied, "My precious, precious child, I love you and I would never leave you! During your times of trial and suffering when you see only one set of footprints, it was then that I <u>carrie</u>d you."

Carolyn Joyce Carty American Poet

Made in the USA
Charleston, SC
21 June 2011